W9-ARH-171

Ancient Wisdom, Timeless Truths

Immortal Philosophers
Discuss the Meaning of Life

Ancient Wisdom, Timeless Truths

Immortal Philosophers Discuss the Meaning of Life

Edited by Jude Patterson

BARNES & NOBLE BOOKS

NEW YORK

The quotes in this book have been drawn from many sources, and are assumed to be accurate as quoted in their previously published forms. Although every effort has been made to verify the quotes and sources, the publisher cannot guarantee their perfect accuracy.

2003 Barnes & Noble Books

ISBN 0-7607-4054-2

Printed and bound in the United States of America

M 9 8 7 6 5 4 3 2

Enlighten me, O Muses, tenants of
Olympian homes,
For you are goddesses, inside on
everything, know everything,
But we mortals hear only the news
and know nothing at all.

—HOMER

Introduction

THE PHILOSOPHERS AND HISTORIANS OF ANCIENT GREECE,
Rome, and China shared one common aim: the search
for truth. Though the Mediterranean and Chinese
cultures were miles apart, their writings explored
universal themes of life and death, war and peace,
the individual and the state, fortune and opportunity,
and above all, vice and virtue—a code of ethics to guide
them in obtaining wisdom and happiness. Then as
now, truth could be found in antiquity—in the wisdom
handed down from generation to generation.

It was in the classical age that the wisdom which
had hitherto been transmitted solely through the oral
tradition of storytelling was recorded and preserved
for all time in writing. Events of the day were also
recorded, and opinions expressed. There were no
newspapers, so news traveled by word of mouth.
Socrates, a stonemason by trade but a philosopher
by natural inclination, engaged the citizens of Athens
in public question-and-answer discussions, which
his pupil Plato later recorded in the dialogues. In
China, the wandering scholar Confucius taught that
learning and meditation put one in harmony with
the order of the universe, and that benevolence was

the key to peace. Like Plato, his disciples preserved his wisdom in the *Analects.* These and other works of the classical age have endured because of their timeless appeal.

Ancient Wisdom, Timeless Truths brings together seventy-eight immortal philosophers and thinkers of the classical age—historians, statesmen, militarists, monarchs, poets, dramatists, and satirists—to point the way toward truth. The issues of their time resonate even today: Plato argues for participation in government; Cicero cautions against gifts to political candidates; Sun-tzu recommends winning wars without hostilities; Confucius offers career guidance; Plutarch emphasizes the importance of character; Socrates awakens the inner guide of conscience; Seneca extols the benefits of meditation and self-reflection; Horace praises the pleasures of friendship and home; Chuang-tzu shares his secret of happiness. The quotes are strung together like a dialogue, and while the conversation is invented, every line is true to its source. So pull up a chair and let time be suspended as you listen in on this discussion of the meaning of life.

Jude Patterson

The Philosophers

Aeschylus (526-456 B.C.), Greek tragic poet

Aesop (6th century B.C.), legendary Greek fabulist

Agathon (c. 445-c. 400 B.C.), Athenian tragic poet and friend of Socrates

Agesilaus II (c. 444-360 B.C.), king of Sparta and commander of Spartan forces

Anacreon (c. 582-c. 485 B.C.), Greek lyric poet

Anaximander of Miletus (610-c. 547 B.C.), Greek astronomer and philosopher

Antiphanes (c. 388-c. 311 B.C.), Greek comic playwright

Archilochus (7th century B.C.), Greek lyric poet

Aristophanes (c. 450-c. 388 B.C.), Athenian comic playwright

Aristotle (384-322 B.C.), Greek philosopher who shaped scientific thinking

Bias (6th century B.C.), one of the Seven Sages of Greece

Bion of Borsythenes (c. 325-c. 255 B.C.), Greek philosopher and satirist

Caecilius Statius (c. 219-166 B.C.), Roman comic poet

Julius Caesar (100-44 B.C.), Roman statesman and general

Cato the Elder (234-149 B.C.), Roman politician and historian

Cato the Younger (95-46 B.C.), Roman politician and great-grandson of Cato the Elder

Catullus (c. 84-c. 54 B.C.), Roman lyric poet

Chabrias (d. c. 357 B.C.), Greek mercenary general

Chuang-tzu (4th century B.C.), Chinese Taoist philosopher

Cicero (106-43 B.C.), Roman statesman, orator, and philosopher

Cleobulus (6th century B.C.), one of the Seven Sages of Greece

Confucius (551-479 B.C.), Chinese ethical philosopher

Croesus (d. c. 546 B.C.), legendary wealthy king of Lydia, in Anatolia

Democritus (c. 460-c. 370 B.C.), Greek atomist philosopher and pupil of Leucippus

Demosthenes (384-322 B.C.), Athenian statesman and orator

Diogenes the Cynic (d. c. 320 B.C.), Greek ascetic philosopher

Quintus Ennius (239-169 B.C.), Roman poet and inventor of shorthand

Epictetus (c. A.D. 55-c. 135), Greek Stoic philosopher

Epicurus (341-270 B.C.), Greek atomist philosopher who believed pleasure is the only good

Euripides (c. 484-406 B.C.), Greek dramatist and tragic poet

Quintus Fabius Cunctator (c. 275-203 B.C.), Roman dictator and general

Heraclitus (c. 540-c. 480 B.C.), Greek metaphysical philosopher

Herodotus (c. 484-c. 425 B.C.), Greek historian known as the "Father of History"

Hesiod (fl. 8th century B.C.), Greek poet, farmer, and genealogist of the gods

Homer (c. 8th century B.C.), Greek epic poet

Horace (65-8 B.C.), Roman poet and satirist

Juvenal (c. A.D. 60-c. 127), Roman satirist and friend of Martial

Lao-tzu (6th century B.C.), Chinese philosopher who founded Taoism

Leucippus (5th century B.C.), Greek philosopher who originated atomistic theory

Livy (59 B.C.-A.D. 17), Roman historian

Lucan (A.D. 39-65), Roman epic poet

Lucretius (c. 98-c. 55 B.C.), Roman Epicurean philosopher and poet

Marcus Aurelius (A.D. 121-180), Roman emperor and Stoic philosopher

Martial (c. A.D. 40-c. 103), Spanish-Roman poet and satirical epigrammatist

Menander (342-292 B.C.), Athenian comic playwright

Mencius (c. 371-c. 289 B.C.), Chinese philosopher and pupil of Confucius

Mimnermus (fl. c. 630 B.C.), Greek elegiac poet

Cornelius Nepos (c. 100-c. 25 B.C.), Roman historian and friend of Catullus and Cicero

Ovid (43 B.C.-A.D. 17), Roman elegiac/erotic poet

Petronius Arbiter (d. A.D. 66), Roman writer and courtier

Phaedrus (5th century B.C.), Greek philosopher and namesake of one of Plato's dialogues

Pindar (c. 522-c. 438 B.C.), Greek lyric poet

Plato (c. 428-c. 347 B.C.), Greek idealist philosopher, pupil of Socrates, and teacher of Aristotle

Plautus (c. 254-184 B.C.), Roman comic playwright

Pliny the Elder (A.D. 23-79), Roman scholar and naturalist

Pliny the Younger (c. A.D. 62–c. 113), Roman statesman, writer, and nephew of Pliny the Elder

Plutarch (c. A.D. 46–c. 120), Greek biographer

Polybius (c. 200–c. 118 B.C.), Greek historian who chronicled Roman conquest

Sextus Propertius (c. 50–c. 15 B.C.), Roman elegiac poet

Ptolemy (c. A.D. 100–c. 170), Roman astronomer and mathematician

Publilius Syrus (1st century B.C.), Roman mime

Pythagoras (c. 580–c. 500 B.C.), Greek philosopher and mathematician

Sallust (c. 86–c. 34 B.C.), Roman politician and historian

Scipio Africanus the Elder (c. 236–c. 183 B.C.), Roman general

Seneca the Younger (c. 4 B.C.–A.D. 65), Spanish-Roman Stoic philosopher, tutor of Nero, and uncle of Lucan

Socrates (c. 470–399 B.C.), Greek philosopher who shaped Western philosophy

Solon (c. 630–c. 560 B.C.), one of the Seven Sages of Greece

Sophocles (c. 496–406 B.C.), Greek tragic dramatist

Sun-tzu (4th century B.C.), Chinese general

Tacitus (c. A.D. 56–c. 120), Roman politician and historian

Terence (c. 185–c. 159 B.C.), Greek-born Roman comic playwright

Themistocles (c. 524–c. 460 B.C.), Athenian military leader and statesman

Theocritus (c. 310–250 B.C.), Greek poet

Thucydides (d. c. 401 B.C.), Athenian military leader and historian

Virgil (70–19 B.C.), Roman poet

Xenocrates (396–314 B.C.), Greek philosopher and pupil of Plato

Xenophon (c. 431–c. 352 B.C.), Greek historian, soldier, and pupil of Socrates

Zeno of Citium (c. 335–c. 263 B.C.), Greek philosopher who founded Stoic school

The Gift of
Philosophy

PLATO: Our discussion is about no ordinary matter, but on the right way to conduct our lives.

SENECA: Life is a gift of the immortal gods, but living well is the gift of philosophy.

CICERO: Socrates was the first to call philosophy down from the heavens and to place it in cities, and even to introduce it into homes and compel it to inquire about life and standards and goods and evils.

PLATO: He said: Who then are the true philosophers?
Those, I said, who are lovers of the vision of truth.

SOCRATES: Philosophy begins in wonder.

SENECA: Truth will never be discovered if we rest contented with discoveries already made.

EPICTETUS: What is the first business of him who philosophizes? To throw away self-conceit. For it is impossible for a man to begin to learn that which he thinks he knows.

SOCRATES: There is only one good, that is, knowledge; and only one evil, that is, ignorance.

POLYBIUS: The knowledge gained from history is the truest education and training for political action.

THUCYDIDES: History is philosophy teaching by examples.

CICERO: History is the witness that testifies to the passing of time; it illumines reality, vitalizes memory, provides guidance in daily life, and brings us tidings of antiquity.

CONFUCIUS: I am not one who was born in the possession of knowledge; I am one who is fond of antiquity, and earnest in seeking it there.

HORACE: The centuries roll back to the ancient age of gold.

SENECA: Believe me, that was a happy age, before the days of architects, before the days of builders.

VIRGIL: I feel again a spark of that ancient flame.

LAO-TZU: To know…the beginning of antiquity Is called the thread running through the Way.

ARISTOTLE: Poetry is something more philosophical and more worthy of serious attention than history, for while poetry is concerned with universal truth, history treats of particular facts.

HERACLITUS: Men who wish to know about the world must learn about it in its particular details.

DEMOCRITUS: The first principles of the universe are atoms and empty space; everything else is merely thought to exist.

LEUCIPPUS: The worlds are formed when atoms fall into the void and are entangled with one another; and from their motion as they increase in bulk, arises the substance of the atoms.

ANAXIMANDER: Living creatures arose from the moist element as it was evaporated by the sun. Man was like another animal, namely a fish, in the beginning.

HORACE: So that what is a beautiful woman on top ends in a black and ugly fish.

ARISTOTLE: Wit is educated insolence.

HORACE: Mix a little foolishness with your prudence: it's good to be silly at the right moment.

HESIOD: Observe due measure, for right timing is in all things the most important factor.

PUBLILIUS SYRUS: While we stop to think, we often miss our opportunity.

PHAEDRUS: Once lost, Jupiter himself cannot bring back opportunity.

CATULLUS: What is given by the gods more desirable than the fortunate hour?

HERODOTUS: Men are dependent on circumstances, not circumstances on men.

LUCRETIUS: The first beginnings of things cannot be distinguished by the eye.

PLATO: The beginning is the most important part of the work.

VIRGIL: Look with favor upon a bold beginning.

ARISTOTLE: Well begun is half done.

LAO-TZU: A journey of a thousand miles must begin with a single step.

VIRGIL: Let us go singing as far as we go: the road will be less tedious.

The Political
Animal

ARISTOTLE: Man is by nature a political animal.

ARISTOPHANES: Under every stone lurks a politician.

ARISTOTLE: If liberty and equality, as is thought by some, are chiefly to be found in democracy, they will be best attained when all persons alike share in the government to the utmost.

SOCRATES: I am not an Athenian or a Greek, but a citizen of the world.

CICERO: The wise man loves not to thrust himself of his own accord into the administration of public affairs, but ..., if circumstances oblige him to it, then he does not refuse the office.

PLATO: The punishment which the wise suffer who refuse to take part in the government, is to live under the government of worse men.

MENCIUS: It is not difficult to govern. All one has to do is not to offend the noble families.

SOCRATES: I was really too honest a man to be a politician and live.

JUVENAL: I refuse to become / An accomplice in theft—which means that no governor / Will accept me on his staff.

CICERO: No one should give or receive a present either during a candidacy or during or after a term of office.

CONFUCIUS: A superior man in dealing with the world is not for anything or against anything. He follows righteousness as the standard.

QUINTUS FABIUS: To be turned from one's course by men's opinions, by blame, and by misrepresentation shows a man unfit to hold an office.

LAO-TZU: The virtuous man promotes agreement; the vicious man allots the blame.

SENECA: You learn to know a pilot in a storm.

PUBLILIUS SYRUS: Anyone can hold the helm when the sea is calm.

SENECA: One must steer, not talk.

PLATO: The state in which the rulers are most reluctant to govern is always the best and most quietly governed, and the state in which they are most eager, the worst.

CONFUCIUS: When the multitude hate a man, it is necessary to examine into the case. When the multitude like a man, it is necessary to examine into the case.

DEMOSTHENES: There is nothing, absolutely nothing, which needs to be more carefully guarded against than that one man should be allowed to become more powerful than the people.

MENCIUS: The people are the most important element in a nation; the spirits of the land and grain are next; the sovereign is the lightest.

CONFUCIUS: Good government obtains when those who are near are made happy, and those who are far off are attracted.

ARISTOTLE: There are two parts of good government: one is the actual obedience of citizens to the laws, the other part is the goodness of the laws which they obey.

CICERO: Justice consists in doing no injury to men; decency in giving them no offense.

TACITUS: The more corrupt the state the more numerous the laws.

ARISTOTLE: Even when laws have been written down, they ought not always to remain unaltered.

CICERO: The good of the people is the greatest law.

MARCUS AURELIUS: That which is not good for the beehive cannot be good for the bees.

PLATO: The first and highest form of the state and of the government and of the law is that in which there prevails most widely the ancient saying, that "Friends have all things in common."

Calumny and Conscience

PUBLILIUS SYRUS: Speech is a mirror of the soul: as a man speaks, so is he.

CHUANG-TZU: Great wisdom is generous; petty wisdom contentious. Great speech is impassioned, small speech cantankerous.

PLATO: Wise men talk because they have something to say; fools because they have to say something.

ZENO: The reason why we have two ears and only one mouth is that we may listen the more and talk the less.

XENOCRATES: I have often repented speaking, but never of holding my tongue.

HORACE: Once a word has been allowed to escape, it cannot be recalled.

TACITUS: It is the rare fortune of these days that one may think what one likes and say what one thinks.

MENANDER: I call a fig a fig, a spade a spade.

SENECA: Let us say what we feel, and feel what we say; let speech harmonize with life.

HOMER: Hateful to me as the gates of Hades is that man who hides one thing in his heart and speaks another.

PLATO: False words are not only evil in themselves, but they infect the soul with evil.

HESIOD: Gossip is mischievous, light and easy to raise, but grievous to bear and hard to get rid of. No gossip ever dies away entirely, if many people voice it: it too is a kind of divinity.

HERODOTUS: A man calumniated is doubly injured—first by him who utters the calumny, and then by him who believes it.

PLAUTUS: Slander-mongers and those who listen to slander, if I had my way, would all be strung up, the talkers by the tongue, the listeners by the ears.

CICERO: Let the punishment match the offense.

JUVENAL: This is the first of punishments, that no guilty man is acquitted if judged by himself.

POLYBIUS: There is no witness so dreadful, no accuser so terrible as the conscience that dwells in the heart of every man.

SOCRATES: This sign, which is a kind of voice, first began to come to me when I was a child; it always forbids but never commands me to do anything which I am going to do.

MENANDER: Conscience is a god to all mortals.

HOMER: All men have need of the gods.

OVID: It is convenient that there be gods, and, as it is convenient, let us believe that there are.

PLATO: Is that which is holy loved by the gods because it is holy, or is it holy because it is loved by the gods?

LUCAN: Is the dwelling place of God anywhere but in the earth and sea, the air and sky, and virtue? Why seek we further for deities? Whatever you see, whatever you touch, that is Jupiter.

SENECA: For what else is Nature but God and the Divine Reason that pervades the whole universe and all its parts?

CHUANG-TZU: If the Universe is hidden in the universe itself, then there can be no escape from it. This is the great truth of things in general.

AESCHYLUS: Zeus, first cause, prime mover; for what thing without Zeus is done among mortals?

PINDAR: If any man hopes to do a deed without God's knowledge, he errs.

HOMER: The gods, likening themselves to all kinds of strangers, go in various disguises from city to city, observing the wrongdoing and the righteousness of men.

SENECA: Live among men as if God beheld you; speak to God as if men were listening.

MARCUS AURELIUS: Live with the gods.

HOMER: Whoever obeys the gods, to him they particularly listen.

LAO-TZU: God's Way is gain that works no harm.

MARCUS AURELIUS: Let every action aim solely at the common good.

PYTHAGORAS: Think before you act.

CONFUCIUS: What you do not want done to yourself, do not do to others.

EPICURUS: Let nothing be done in your life which will cause you fear if it becomes known to your neighbor.

LUCRETIUS: Violence and injury enclose in their net all that do such things, and generally return upon him who began.

SENECA: To be feared is to fear: no one has been able to strike terror into others and at the same time enjoy peace of mind himself.

EURIPIDES: The common interests / of states and individuals alike demand / that good and evil receive their just rewards.

SOCRATES: We ought not to retaliate or render evil for evil to anyone, whatever evil we may have suffered from him.

PLATO: Of all the things of a man's soul which he has within him, justice is the greatest good and injustice the greatest evil.

CONFUCIUS: Recompense injury with justice, and recompense kindness with kindness.

LAO-TZU: To the good I would be good; to the not-good I would also be good, in order to make them good.

PETRONIUS ARBITER: One good turn deserves another.

The Art of War

SENECA: We are mad, not only individually, but nationally. We check manslaughter and isolated murders; but what of war and the much vaunted crime of slaughtering whole peoples?

ARISTOTLE: We make war that we may live in peace.

THUCYDIDES: War is an evil thing; but to submit to the dictation of other states is worse.

MENCIUS: If you know that [a] thing is unrighteous, then use all dispatch in putting an end to it—why wait till next year?

SUN-TZU: The best victory is when the opponent surrenders of its own accord before there are any actual hostilities. . . . It is best to win without fighting.

TERENCE: He is wise who tries everything before arms.

MENANDER: The man who runs may fight again.

PLUTARCH: Where the lion's skin will not reach, you must patch it out with the fox's.

CHABRIAS: An army of deer led by a lion is more to be feared than an army of lions led by a deer.

TACITUS: Courage is the peculiar excellence of man, and the gods help the braver side.

AGESILAUS: A general needs to show daring towards his opponents, good will towards his subordinates and a cool head in crises.

PLUTARCH: Whenever [Agesilaus] wanted some job done promptly by his troops, he first got down to it personally in full view of everyone.

LIVY: No other general was ever more familiar with his soldiers; [Valerius] cheerfully shared all the fatigues with the lowest of his men.

PLUTARCH: Caesar … above all men was gifted with the faculty of making the right use of everything in war, and most especially of seizing the right moment.

SUN-TZU: He whose generals are able and not interfered with by the sovereign will be victorious.

THEMISTOCLES: He who commands the sea has command of everything.

LAO-TZU: One who is good at being a warrior does not appear formidable.

SUN-TZU: Be extremely subtle, even to the point of formlessness. Be extremely mysterious, even to the point of soundlessness. Thereby you can be the director of the opponent's fate.

POLYBIUS: Those who know how to win are much more numerous than those who know how to make proper use of their victories.

SCIPIO AFRICANUS: The Romans do not lose their courage in defeat, nor does victory make them overbearing.

ARISTOTLE: War compels men to be just and temperate, whereas the enjoyment of good fortune and the leisure which comes with peace tends to make them insolent.

JUVENAL: The evils of too-long peace. Luxury, deadlier / Than any armed invader.

CROESUS: No one is so foolish as to prefer to peace war, in which, instead of sons burying their fathers, fathers bury their sons.

HORACE: It is sweet and honorable to die for one's country.

TACITUS: When Vitellius was dead, the war had indeed come to an end, but peace had yet to begin. Sword in hand, throughout the capital, the conquerors hunted down the conquered with merciless hatred. The streets were choked with carnage.... But the ferocity, which in the first impulse of hatred could be gratified only by blood, soon passed into the greed of gain.

SOCRATES: Wars are occasioned by the love of money.

CICERO: The sinews of war, a limitless supply of money.

PUBLILIUS SYRUS: Money alone sets all the world in motion.

Desire

PLATO: Oligarchy: A government resting on a valuation of property, in which the rich have power and the poor man is deprived of it.

ARISTOTLE: The best political community is formed by citizens of the middle class.

CONFUCIUS: When a country is well governed, poverty and a mean condition are things to be ashamed of. When a country is ill governed, riches and honor are things to be ashamed of.

PLATO: Wealth is the parent of luxury and indolence, and poverty of meanness and viciousness, and both of discontent.

ARISTOTLE: Poverty is the parent of revolution and crime.

ARISTOPHANES: We say that poverty is the sister of beggary.

THUCYDIDES: The real disgrace of poverty [is] not in owning to the fact but in declining the struggle against it.

HORACE: Barefaced poverty drove me to writing verses.

JUVENAL: We all live in a state of ambitious poverty.

HORACE: We are just statistics, born to consume resources.

CATO THE ELDER: Even though work stops, expenses run on.

SOCRATES: Virtue does not come from money, but from virtue comes money and all other good things to man, both to the individual and to the state.

HORACE: Citizens, citizens, the first thing to acquire is money. Cash before conscience!

HESIOD: Shun evil profit, for dishonest gain
Is just the same as failure.

JUVENAL: The stink of profit is sweet / Whatever
its source.

CICERO: I do not . . . find fault with the accumu-
lation of property, provided it hurts nobody, but
unjust acquisition of it is always to be avoided.

PLAUTUS: There are occasions when it is
undoubtedly better to incur loss than to
make gain.

PETRONIUS ARBITER: One man will tell you one
rule of life, and another'll tell you another. But *I*
say, "Buy cheap and sell dear," and so you see
I'm bursting with wealth.

BION: He has not acquired a fortune; the fortune
has acquired him.

CICERO: There is nothing so characteristic of narrowness and littleness of soul as the love of riches.

ARISTOTLE: A good life requires a supply of external goods, in a less degree when men are in a good state, in a greater degree when they are in a lower state.

HORACE: The covetous man is ever in want.

SENECA: We often want one thing and pray for another, not telling the truth even to the gods.

AESOP: We would often be sorry if our wishes were gratified.

QUINTUS ENNIUS: The idle mind knows not what it is it wants.

THEMISTOCLES: I prefer a man without money to money without a man.

PUBLILIUS SYRUS: A good reputation is more valuable than money.

ANTIPHANES: We must have richness of soul.

JUVENAL: A sound mind in a sound body.

SENECA: The soul is not disfigured by the ugliness of the body, but rather the opposite, that the body is beautified by the comeliness of the soul.

PLUTARCH: Beauty is the flower of virtue.

CICERO: I like myself, but I won't say I'm as handsome as the bull that kidnapped Europa.

JUVENAL: A hairy body, and arms stiff with bristles, give promise of a manly soul.

VIRGIL: Don't bank too much on your complexion, lovely boy.

THEOCRITUS: Our concern be peace of mind: some old crone let us seek, / To spit on us for luck and keep unlovely things afar.

Linger in Your
Own Company

SOCRATES: Why do you wonder that globe-trotting does not help you, seeing that you always take yourself with you? The reason which set you wandering is ever at your heels.

HORACE: They change their clime, not their disposition, who run across the sea.

SENECA: The evil which assails us is not in the localities we inhabit but in ourselves. We lack strength to endure the least task, being incapable of suffering pain, powerless to enjoy pleasure, impatient with everything. How many invoke death when, after having tried every sort of change, they find themselves reverting to the same sensations, unable to discover any new experience.

SOPHOCLES: When a man has lost all happiness, / he's not alive. Call him a breathing corpse.

HERACLITUS: To do the same thing over and over again is not only boredom: it is to be controlled by rather than to control what you do.

PYTHAGORAS: The greatest strength and wealth is self-control.

SENECA: The primary indication ... of a well-ordered mind is a man's ability to remain in one place and linger in his own company.

MARCUS AURELIUS: Nowhere can a man find a quieter or more untroubled retreat than in his own soul.

PLATO: I must first know myself, as the Delphian inscription says; to be curious about that which is not my concern, while I am still in ignorance of my own self, would be ridiculous.

LAO-TZU: He who knows others is wise;
He who knows himself is enlightened.

SOCRATES: The unexamined life is not worth living.

PUBLILIUS SYRUS: Wisdom is acquired by meditation.

SENECA: Every day I plead my cause before the bar of self. When the light has been removed from sight, and my wife, long aware of my habit, has become silent, I scan the whole of my day and retrace all my deeds and words. I conceal nothing from myself, I omit nothing. For why should I shrink from any of my mistakes, when I may commune thus with myself.

ARISTOTLE: The good man is glad to hold converse with himself, for he has pleasant memories of the past and fair hopes for the future, on which he can dwell with satisfaction; nor has he any lack of topics upon which to exercise the speculative powers of his mind.

CHUANG-TZU: Cherish that which is within you, and shut off that which is without; for much knowledge is a curse.

SENECA: [Demetrius the Cynic says that it] is far better for us to possess only a few maxims of philosophy that are nevertheless always at our command and in use than to acquire vast knowledge that notwithstanding serves no useful purpose.

LAO-TZU: Let people hold on to these:
Manifest plainness,
Embrace simplicity,
Reduce selfishness,
Have few desires.

MENCIUS: There is nothing better for the nurturing of the heart than to reduce the number of one's desires.

XENOPHON: To want nothing is godlike; and the less we want the nearer we approach the divine.

CHUANG-TZU: My greatest happiness consists precisely in doing nothing whatever that is calculated to obtain happiness.

The Circle of
Friendship

CICERO: The shifts of Fortune test the reliability of friends.

OVID: So long as you are secure you will count many friends; if your life becomes clouded you will be alone.

EURIPIDES: Blood's thicker than water, and when one's in trouble / Best to seek out a relative's open arms.

TERENCE: Charity begins at home.

PLINY THE YOUNGER: Home is where the heart is.

CICERO: What is more agreeable than one's home?

HORACE: The smoke, the wealth, the noise of Rome!

ARISTOPHANES: A man's homeland is wherever he prospers.

ARISTOTLE: Without friends no one would choose to live, though he had all other goods.

PLAUTUS: Nothing is there more friendly to a man than a friend in need.

MARTIAL: Property given away to friends is the only kind that will forever be yours.

PYTHAGORAS: Friends share all things.

PLATO: [Recall] the ancient saying, that "Friends have all things in common."

DEMOCRITUS: Similarity of outlook creates friendship.

SALLUST: To like and dislike the same things, that is indeed true friendship.

CICERO: A friend is, as it were, a second self.

HORACE: The half of my own soul.

ARISTOTLE: What is a friend? A single soul dwelling in two bodies.

CICERO: To give and receive advice—the former with freedom and yet without bitterness, the latter with patience and without irritation—is peculiarly appropriate to genuine friendship.

CATO THE YOUNGER: Some men are better served by their bitter-tongued enemies than by their sweet-smiling friends, because the former often tell the truth, the latter, never.

ARISTOPHANES: The wise learn many things from their enemies.

DEMOCRITUS: The enmity of one's kindred is far more bitter than the enmity of strangers.

PTOLEMY: There are three classes of friendship and enmity, since men are so disposed to one another either by preference or by need or through pleasure and pain.

CLEOBULUS: We should render a service to a friend to bind him closer to us, and to an enemy in order to make a friend of him.

PLINY THE YOUNGER: The first essential is to be content with your own lot; the second, to support and assist those you know to be most in need, embracing them all within the circle of your friendship.

SENECA: Indeed ... [a person who has begun to be a friend to himelf] can never be alone. You may be sure that such a man is a friend to all mankind.

MENCIUS: Try your best to treat others as you wish to be treated yourself, and you will find that this is the shortest way to benevolence.

PUBLILIUS SYRUS: What is it to practice benevolence? It is to imitate the Deity.

PLATO: Love … has the greatest power, and is the source of all our happiness and harmony, and makes us friends with the gods who are above us, and with one another.

MARCUS AURELIUS: It is man's peculiar duty to love even those who wrong him.

VIRGIL: I have known sorrow and learned to aid the wretched.

AESOP: No act of kindness, no matter how small, is ever wasted.

VIRGIL: Love conquers all things; let us too surrender to Love.

Do What You Would Be

ZENO: Fortune bids me to follow philosophy with fewer encumbrances.

LUCRETIUS: If a man would guide his life by true philosophy, he will find ample riches in a modest livelihood enjoyed with a tranquil mind.

MENCIUS: Men must be decided on what they will not do, and then they are able to act with vigor in what they ought to do.

DEMOSTHENES: You cannot have a proud and chivalrous spirit if your conduct is mean and paltry; for whatever a man's actions are, such must be his spirit.

ARISTOTLE: Virtue is more clearly shown in the performance of fine actions than in the nonperformance of base ones.

TACITUS: His character was of an average kind, rather free from vices than distinguished by virtues.

CONFUCIUS: In ancient times, men learned with a view to their own improvement. Nowadays, men learn with a view to the approbation of others.

TACITUS: The desire for glory clings even to the best men longer than any other passion.

SENECA: You can tell the character of every man when you see how he receives praise.

BIAS: When you do well, do not praise yourself but the gods.

AESCHYLUS: It is in the character of very few men to honor without envy a friend who has prospered.

PLINY THE YOUNGER: A [noble] spirit will seek the reward of virtue in the consciousness of it, rather than in popular opinion.

CONFUCIUS: A man should say, ... I am not concerned that I am not known, I seek to be worthy to be known.

HORACE: For joys fall not to the rich alone, nor has he lived ill who from birth to death has passed unknown.

VIRGIL: We are not all capable of everything.

HOMER: So it is that the gods do not give all men gifts of grace—neither good looks nor intelligence nor eloquence.

PUBLILIUS SYRUS: You are eloquent enough if truth speaks through you.

HOMER: The fates have given mankind a patient soul.

PLAUTUS: Patience is the best remedy for every trouble.

SENECA: At our birth nature ... gave us reason, not perfect, but capable of being perfected.

ARISTOTLE: Reason is a light that God has kindled in the soul.

SOCRATES: If the truth of all things always existed in the soul, then the soul is immortal. Wherefore be of good cheer, and try to recollect what you do not know, or rather what you do not remember.

PYTHAGORAS: Reason is immortal, all else mortal.

CICERO: A strong argument that men's knowledge antedates their birth is the fact that mere children, in studying difficult subjects, so quickly lay hold upon innumerable things that they seem not to be ... learning ... for the first time, but to be recalling.

SALLUST: The renown which riches or beauty confer is fleeting and frail; ... the splendid achievements of the intellect, like the soul, are everlasting.

CONFUCIUS: By nature, men are nearly alike; by practice, they get to be wide apart.

SEXTUS PROPERTIUS: Let each man pass his days in that wherein his skill is greatest.

CONFUCIUS: Choose a job you love, and you will never have to work a day in your life.

EPICTETUS: First say to yourself what you would be; and then do what you have to do.

VIRGIL: Practice and thought might gradually forge many an art.

PLUTARCH: Character is simply habit long continued.

OVID: Nothing is stronger than habit.

HESIOD: If you add a little to a little, and then do it again, soon that little shall be much.

CONFUCIUS: Trickling water, if not stopped, will become a mighty river.

MENANDER: When good character adds adornment to natural charms, whoever comes near is doubly captivated.

HERACLITUS: A man's character is his fate.

HORACE: It is not the rich man you should properly call happy, but him who knows how to use with wisdom the blessings of the gods, to endure hard poverty, and who fears dishonor worse than death, and is not afraid to die for cherished friends or fatherland.

PLINY THE YOUNGER: The fortunate man...is he to whom the gods have granted the power either to do something which is worth recording or to write what is worth reading, and most fortunate of all is the man who can do both.

MENCIUS: The great man is he who does not lose his child's-heart.

VIRGIL: Good speed to your youthful valor, boy! So shall you scale the stars!

The Unbent Mind

PLINY THE ELDER: In comparing various authors with one another, I have discovered that some of the gravest and latest writers have transcribed, word for word, from former works, without making acknowledgment.

SENECA: Whatever is well said by another, is mine.

TERENCE: In fact, nothing is said that has not been said before.

PLUTARCH: I am writing biography,... and the truth is that the most brilliant exploits [in history] often tell us nothing of the virtues or vices of the men who performed them, while on the other hand a chance remark or a joke may reveal far more of a man's character than the mere feat of winning battles in which thousands fall, or of marshaling great armies, or laying siege to cities.

SENECA: I have withdrawn not only from men, but from affairs; I am working for later generations, writing down some ideas that may be of assistance to them.

LUCRETIUS: On a dark theme I trace verses full of light, touching all the Muses' charm.

VIRGIL: Me too the Muses made write verse. I have songs of my own, the shepherds call me also a poet; but I'm not inclined to trust them. For I don't seem yet to write things as good either as Varius or as Cinna, but to be a goose honking amongst tuneful swans.

PUBLILIUS SYRUS: It takes a long time to bring excellence to maturity.

MARTIAL: Some good, some so-so, and lots plain bad: that's how a book of poems is made, my friend.

CATULLUS: To whom am I to present my pretty new book, freshly smoothed off with dry pumice stone? To you, Cornelius: for you used to think that my trifles were worth something, long ago.

CORNELIUS NEPOS: Tasteful rather than expensive.

JUVENAL: Many suffer from the incurable disease of writing, and it becomes chronic in their sick minds.

QUINTUS ENNIUS: I never indulge in poetics Unless I am down with rheumatics.

SOCRATES: I soon made up my mind about the poets. . . . I decided that it was not wisdom that enabled them to write their poetry, but a kind of instinct or inspiration, such as you find in seers and prophets who deliver all their sublime messages without knowing in the least what they mean.

AGATHON: Everyone becomes a poet whom Love touches.

MARTIAL: My poems are naughty, but my life is pure.

HORACE: No poems can please for long or live that are written by water-drinkers.

ARISTOPHANES: Quickly, bring me a beaker of wine, so that I may wet my mind and say something clever.

HORACE: It is sweet to let the mind unbend on occasion.

SOLON: Let us sacrifice to the Muses.

ARISTOPHANES: When men drink, then they are rich and successful and win lawsuits and are happy and help their friends.

HERODOTUS: Success for the most part attends those who act boldly, not those who weigh everything, and are [slow] to venture.

ARISTOPHANES: A woman's time of opportunity is short, and if she doesn't seize it, no one wants to marry her, and she sits watching for omens.

CICERO: It was ordained at the beginning of the world that certain signs should prefigure certain events.

PLINY THE ELDER: When a building is about to fall down, all the mice desert it.

PLAUTUS: Consider the little mouse, how sagacious an animal it is which never entrusts its life to one hole only.

HORACE: Let me remind you what the wary fox said once upon a time to the sick lion: "Because those footprints scare me, all directed your way, none coming back."

AESOP: It is easier to get into the enemy's toils than out again.

PHAEDRUS: It has been related that dogs drink at the river Nile running along, that they may not be seized by the crocodiles.

ARISTOPHANES: There is no animal more invincible than a woman, nor fire either, nor any wildcat so ruthless.

MIMNERMUS: What life is there, what delight, without golden Aphrodite?

MENANDER: A chaste woman ought not to dye her hair yellow.

ARCHILOCHUS: Old women should not seek to be perfumed.

PLUTARCH: When the candles are out all women are fair.

ANACREON: Bring water, bring wine, boy! Bring flowering garlands to me! Yes, bring them, so that I may try a bout with love.

MARTIAL: You ask what a nice girl will do? She won't give an inch, but she won't say no.

CAECILIUS STATIUS: She'd have you spew up what you've drunk when you were out.

MARTIAL: [She's] obstinate, pliant, merry, morose, all at once. For me there's no living with [her], or without [her].

ARISTOPHANES: These impossible women! How they do get around us! / The poet was right: can't live with them, or without them!

OVID: Love yields to business. If you seek a way out of love, be busy; you'll be safe then.

HOMER: The wine urges me on, the bewitching wine, which sets even a wise man to singing and to laughing gently and rouses him up to dance and brings forth words which were better unspoken.

PLAUTUS: To blow and swallow at the same moment is not easy.

HORACE: Now is the time for drinking, now the time to beat the earth with unfettered foot.

DIOGENES THE CYNIC: Discourse on virtue and they pass by in droves, whistle and dance the shimmy, and you've got an audience.

JUVENAL: Two things only the people anxiously desire, / Bread and the Circus games.

CATULLUS: Oh this age! How tasteless and ill-bred it is!

The Torch
of Life

PTOLEMY: The length of life takes the leading place among inquiries about events following birth.

SENECA: Men do not care how nobly they live, but only how long, although it is within the reach of every man to live nobly, but within no man's power to live long.

MARTIAL: Virtue extends our days: he lives two lives who relives his past with pleasure.

PLATO: He who is of a calm and happy nature will hardly feel the pressure of age, but to him who is of an opposite disposition youth and age are equally a burden.

CICERO: Give me a young man in whom there is something of the old, and an old man with something of the young: guided so, a man may grow old in body, but never in mind.

MENANDER: Whom the gods love dies young.

MARCUS AURELIUS: The longest-lived and the shortest-lived man, when they come to die, lose one and the same thing.

SENECA: Anyone can take life from man, but no one death: a thousand gates stand open to it.

HORACE: Do not try to find out—we're forbidden to know—what end the gods may bestow on me or you.

JULIUS CAESAR: What sort of death is best? A sudden death.

CATULLUS: It is difficult suddenly to lay aside a long-cherished love.

VIRGIL: Here are the tears of things; mortality touches the heart.

HOMER: Thus she spoke; and I longed to embrace my dead mother's ghost. Thrice I tried to clasp her image, and thrice it slipped through my hands, like a shadow, like a dream.

EURIPIDES: A sweet thing, for whatever time,
to revisit in dreams the dear dead we have lost.

SEXTUS PROPERTIUS: There is something beyond
the grave; death does not end all, and the pale
ghost escapes from the vanquished pyre.

SOCRATES: It is perfectly certain that the soul is
immortal and imperishable, and our souls will
actually exist in another world.

CORNELIUS NEPOS: So that he seemed not to
relinquish life, but to leave one home for another.

CICERO: The spirit is the true self.

EPICTETUS: You are a little soul carrying around
a corpse.

LAO-TZU: Not to lose one's station is to endure;
Not to be forgotten when dead is long lived.

TACITUS: Think of your forefathers and posterity.

PUBLILIUS SYRUS: The weeping of an heir is laughter in disguise.

PLUTARCH: It is indeed a desirable thing to be well-descended, but the glory belongs to our ancestors.

VIRGIL: Begin, baby boy: if you haven't had a smile for your parent, then neither will a god think you worth inviting to dinner, nor a goddess to bed.

SOCRATES: Ordinary people seem not to realize that those who really apply themselves in the right way to philosophy are directly and of their own accord preparing themselves for dying and death.

PLATO: You are young, my son, and, as the years go by, time will change and even reverse many of your present opinions. Refrain therefore awhile from setting yourself up as a judge of the highest matters.

MARCUS AURELIUS: The universe is change; our life is what our thoughts make it.

PLUTARCH: Pythagoras, when he was asked what time was, answered that it was the soul of this world.

VIRGIL: Time bears away all things, even our minds.

EURIPIDES: Time will reveal everything; it is a babbler, and speaks even when not asked.

ARISTOTLE: Time crumbles things; everything grows old under the power of Time and is forgotten through the lapse of Time.

PLINY THE ELDER: God has no power over the past except to cover it with oblivion.

AGATHON: This only is denied to God: the power to undo the past.

CONFUCIUS: Things that are done, it is needless to speak about ...; things that are past, it is needless to blame.

OVID: Everything flows onward; all things are brought into being with a changing nature; the ages themselves glide by in constant movement.

LUCRETIUS: Thus the sum of things is ever being renewed, and mortals live dependent one upon another. Some nations increase, others diminish, and in a short space the generations of living creatures are changed and like runners pass on the torch of life.

HORACE: While we're talking, envious time is fleeing: seize the day, put no trust in the future.

CONFUCIUS: Set your will on the Way. Have a firm grasp on virtue. Rely on humanity. Find recreation in the arts.

MARCUS AURELIUS: Death hangs over thee. While thou still live, while thou may, do good.